Kitesurfing

by Stephen Timblin

Published by The Child's World®
1980 Lookout Drive
Mankato, MN 56003-1705
800-599-READ
www.childsworld.com

The Child's World®: Mary Berendes, Publishing Director
Shoreline Publishing Group, LLC: James Buckley Jr.,
  Production Director
The Design Lab: Design and production

ISBN 9781609731830
LCCN 2011928873

Photo credits: Cover: Photos.com.
Interior: Gavin Butler, 25; dreamstime.com: Hasan Can
Balcioglu 11, Alex Bramwell 12, Sailorr 23; Adriene
Freville, 28; Jim Gaunt/F Stop Press: 4; iStock: 16, 20;
Courtesy Bruno Legaignoux: 7; Photos.com: 8, 10, 15,
19; Slingshot Sports: 27

Printed in the United States of America

Table of Contents

Lewis Crathern soars high over a pier in England . . . on a kiteboard!

M.GAUNT/F Stop Press

CHAPTER ONE

Ride the Wind!

Brighton Pier off the coast of southern England is more than 100 years old. It has survived everything from powerful storms to a major fire. The pier is lined with stores, restaurants, and even an amusement park. As Brighton's main tourist attraction, the pier has hosted concerts, festivals, and other events since 1899.

But on November 12, 2010, those lucky enough to be standing on the pier **witnessed** something no one had ever seen before. Powered by winds gusting to more than 60 miles per hour (96 kph), kiteboarder Lewis Crathern launched high off a wave. Riding beneath a large kite-like sail, he soared like a bird *over* the 50-foot-high (15-m-high) pier.

"You only get one try. If you don't get it right, you could die," said the 26-year-old daredevil. He was, not surprisingly, the first person to jump the famed pier. Or was he flying?

Crathern is one of the top riders in the growing sport of kiteboarding, also known as kitesurfing. This awesome sport combines surfing, wind surfing, wakeboarding, and even skateboarding into one extreme adventure.

Who gets the credit for inventing kiteboarding? There's no easy answer to that question. After all, humans have been using wind to sail across water for thousands of years. Kites were commonly flown in ancient China as long as 2,500 years ago. Native Hawaiians have been surfing for centuries.

In the 1980s, Dominique and Bruno Legaignoux were among the first to put these pieces together. Former sailing champions and crafty inventors, the two French brothers began flying giant kites. They rode beneath the kites while on water skis. In 1985, they settled on an inflatable U-shaped kite. They made it inflatable, too, meaning it was partly filled with air. This made it easier to launch off the water, even after it got wet.

Bruno and Domi Legaignoux are still active in the sport they helped invent.

The latest kiteboards let riders fly over waves.

By 1988, the sport's first World Cup was held in Hawaii. Still, there were only a few dozen expert kiteboarders at that time. Riders used boards borrowed from other sports such as surfing. The kites were tricky to launch as well as control once in the air.

As kites and boards improved, the sport grew in popularity. In the 1990s, different riding styles were created. Some riders chose to glide side-by-side with surfers. They aimed for long, smooth runs powered by the wind. Others borrowed freestyle tricks from sports like wakeboarding, snowboarding, and skateboarding. These riders flew high in the air from wave tops before landing with a splash.

Wind and Snow

When thrill-seeking skiers saw kiteboarding, they just had to try it, too—on snow! Almost overnight the sport of snowkiting was born. Most snowkiters stick to frozen lakes, fields, and other flat surfaces, using the wind to glide across the snow. Some extreme riders, however, use their kites to soar down and across mountains. They zip in and out of canyons in thrilling fashion on their way down the mountain.

Today, there are hundreds of thousands of kiteboarders riding the wind around the world. The sight of riders skimming across the water and boosting high into the air thrill beachgoers. Popular kiteboarding spots can be found from San Francisco to Sydney and from Florida to the south of France. Some people are even working to get kiteboarding into the Olympics. That's not bad for a sport that's still being invented every day out on the water!

The Golden Gate Bridge frames this fast-moving kitesurfer in San Francisco.

Some riders need help from the beach when taking off in high winds.

CHAPTER TWO

Kiteboarding Gear and Skills

The key gear for kiteboarding is right there in the name—a kite and a board. And if you began riding twenty years ago when the sport first took off, things were that simple. Boards designed just for kiteboarding didn't exist. Riders used surfboards or wakeboards. Kite designs were extremely basic, with only a few options to choose from.

What a difference a couple decades make! Flip through a kiteboarding magazine today and you'll see ads for dozens of companies offering a wide range of products.

The most important piece of equipment is the kite itself. Some are better for light, medium, or heavy winds. Others are designed for styles such as freestyle, racing, or wave riding.

Kiteboarding beginners all start with a training kite. Knowing how to fly your kite is the single most important skill for the sport. Before ever getting into the water, a kiteboarder must learn to use the wind. The wind gets the kite in the air. Then riders learn how to steer the kite to help them move in whichever direction they can.

Training kites are around 4 feet (1.2 m) wide. They are flown on land like a regular toy kite. Even at that small size, you can feel the force of the wind tugging at you—hard! That's because kiteboarding kites are part of the "power kite" family. They have to be strong to not only fly but pull the kiteboarder on the other end. In training, you get the feeling of what it's like to be below a regular kiteboarding kite that's 30 feet (10 m) wide!

Though large, kites are very lightweight.
Most riders can carry one by themselves.

The foot straps keep the rider from losing the board on jumps like this one.

As with kites, boards come in all shapes and sizes. Wave riders use boards that look a lot like surfboards. They are only going to aim in one direction . . . forward. Freestyle riders hop on twin-tip boards. Having a pointed tip at either end lets them spin easily and ride in either direction. Racing boards are extra narrow, allowing riders to cut through the water more easily at high speeds. As with a surfboard or snowboard, riders also use a leash to attach themselves to the board in case they fall and the board shoots out beneath them. Most riders also put their feet under foot straps. This is especially important for **aerial** tricks so that rider and board stay together!

Two other **vital** pieces of gear are the control bar and **harness**, both of which connect a rider to the kite. Watching a kiteboarder in action makes it look like all the pressure is on his or her arms as they hold onto the kite. In reality, the bar and harness take most of the pull of the kite. Holding on to that much power with just two arms would be very difficult. Rides would be very short. The harness worn by riders lets them focus on controlling the kite rather than just holding it. It also makes it possible to hold on one-handed while doing board grabs and other tricks.

The harness is around the rider's middle. He holds the control bar in front of him.

Depower Generation

The first kiteboards were hard to control. Two simple ropes were all the rider had to steer and stop. Today's boards have as many as five ropes. Along with making launching easier, these extra lines give riders incredible control along with the ability to "depower." They let a rider drop the kite out of the wind immediately. Now kites have brakes!

Leaning to one side helps the rider control her direction and speed.

Once you have your gear, it's time to hit the water. Kiteboarding is a tricky sport to learn. Beginners should start with lessons. Experienced teachers can show you to launch your kite while in the water and to balance on your board.

They will also teach you key safety rules. For example, never launch a kite directly into the wind. This gives the kite power right away. It can yank you into the water and lead to injury. Riders must be in total control and ready to stop at all times. Also, you need to keep clear of other riders to avoid tangling lines or colliding.

The bottom line? Respect your ability, the wind, and other riders. Then you'll have a wonderful day riding the wind!

CHAPTER THREE

Riders and Records

Many of the world's best kiteboarding spots are located beside beautiful beaches. Some of the most famous places include Cabarete in the Dominican Republic and Turks & Caicos Islands. Maui, Hawaii, is the best spot in those islands. In Oregon, the Hood River Gorge provides kitesurfers with some of the steadiest, most powerful winds around.

No matter where you ride, most kiteboarders will tell you that spending a day out on the water with friends is more important than winning a race. For them, the sport simply challenges riders to reach new heights. That might mean learning a new trick, riding faster, or going higher while catching major air.

When the wind is blowing, look for several kitesurfers to hit the waves together.

Kristin Boese is one of the best kitesurfers in the world . . . man or woman!

Here are a few of the top riders who push themselves to take kiteboarding to the next level.

- The Legend: Few riders have done as much for the sport as Pete Cabrinha. Born in Hawaii, Pete has spent the last three decades mastering big-wave surfing, windsurfing, and now kiteboardering. He holds the record for the largest wave ever surfed—a seven-story monster wave off the island of Maui. Cabrinha Kiteboards is one of the largest kiteboarding companies in the world.
- The Champ: In 2009, German kiteboarder Kristin Boese rode herself into the Guinness Book of World Records by winning her record ninth kiteboarding world championship! The key to Kristin's success is her **versatility**—her titles include wins in freestyle, race, and wave competitions.

- The Trick Master: Australian Andy Yates is one of the top freestyle kiteboarders in the world. He was the 2010 Professional Kiteboard Riders Association (PKRA) Freestyle champion. Andy is known for his big bag of tricks. But even Andy admits he has his limits. "No one can do every trick in every aspect of kiteboarding," he says. "That's why the fun and the new ideas never end."

- The Long Distance Rider: The current record holder for longest distance traveled on a kiteboard is American Phil Midler. In 2010, Phil rode for 17 hours straight, traveling an incredible 205.5 nautical miles along the Texas coast.

Andy Yates thrills fans with high-flying flips like this one.

Rob Douglas zooms along the shallow water off Africa to set a world record for speed.

Finally, let's talk about speed! Off the coast of Namibia in Western Africa, winds often blow more than 70 miles per hour (113 kph). The site is perfect for the Luderitz Speed Challenge, named for a nearby village. A special trench was dug offshore to make sure the watery track is as fast as possible. Since 2007, the fastest kiteboarders in the world have challenged the track and themselves.

France's Charlotte Consorti smashed the women's record by reaching 58 mph (93 kph) in 2010. American Rob Douglas holds the men's world record. Rob reached a speed of 65 mph (105 kph) on his racing board at the 2010 Luderitz Speed Challenge.

"It felt like I was driving a car that fast with the top down," said Rob.

Riding for speed, doing tricks, or just feeling the wind in their face, kiteboarders are zooming across waters around the world. They've found another way to "go fly a kite."

Glossary

aerial—happening in the air

harness—the straps a person wears to connect them to something else

versatility—ability to do many things

vital—important

witnessed—saw

Find Out More

BOOKS

Kiteboarding
By Joanne Mattern (Rourke Publishing, 2008)
Another introduction to the sport, including action photos and
information on places to kitesurf.

Kitesurfing in the Waves: The Complete Guide
By Kristin Boese (Wiley, 2009)
This book is aimed at older readers, but it's great if you really want to
find out all you can about kitesurfing—the author is the eight-time world
champion featured on page 25 of our book.

WEB SITES

For links to learn more about extreme sports: **childsworld.com/links**

Note to Parents, Teachers, and Librarians: We routinely verify our Web
links to make sure they are safe and active sites. So encourage your
readers to check them out!

Index

About the Author

When it comes to board sports, **Stephen Timblin** would rather be snowboarding. He has written books for readers of all ages, and enjoys spending time with his beautiful twin daughters.